THE GIGANTIC BEARD THAT WAS EVIL

THE GIGANTIC BEARD THAT WAS EVIL

Stephen Collins

PICADOR

New York

For Hannah

1.

HERE

Beneath the skin

of everything

is something nobody can know.

The job of the skin

is to keep it all in

and never let anything show.

Dave was as smooth as a bowling ball.

(Hence the wig.)

And all his life, Dave had liked to draw his street.

He really

really

really liked drawing his street.

It was just so *neat*. So...

Complete. That's the word.

Complete.

And in the evenings,

when most people were watching television,

or reading newspapers,

or playing video games

Dave would just sit

and look at his street

and draw what he saw.

He thought it was beautiful.

He found a certain comfort
in its tidiness.

Dave's street was certainly tidy.

Not that this was unusual, of course.

Everywhere was impeccably,
impossibly neat.

'Everywhere' was Here. It was a very big island.

Though nobody used the word 'island'.

If they called it anything, they just called it

'Here'.

Here, every tree was perfect.

Every street was perfect.

Even the very *shape* of

HERE

was perfect.

But although Dave's street

was just
as perfect

as every other
part of Here,

nobody *really* wanted to live on it.

FOR SALE

FOR SALE

FOR SALE

Not even the people who lived there.

Not even
Dave.

For much as he loved the street
in front of his house,

he hated what
was behind it.

The sea.

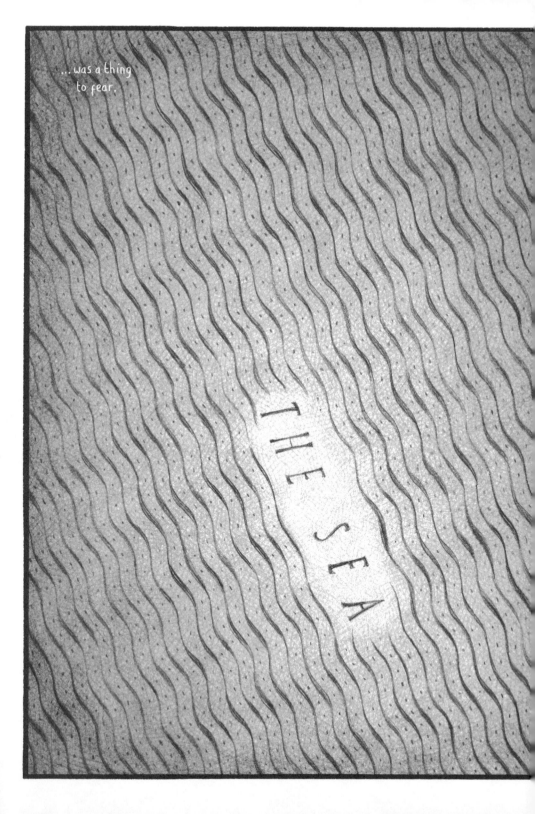

THERE

THE·EDGE·OF·THE·SEA

The sea

led to *There*.

There

There

There

was disorder.

was chaos.

was evil.

In fact, There was a place to which nobody had ever even *been*. No one alive, anyway.
The stories were enough for most people, including Dave.

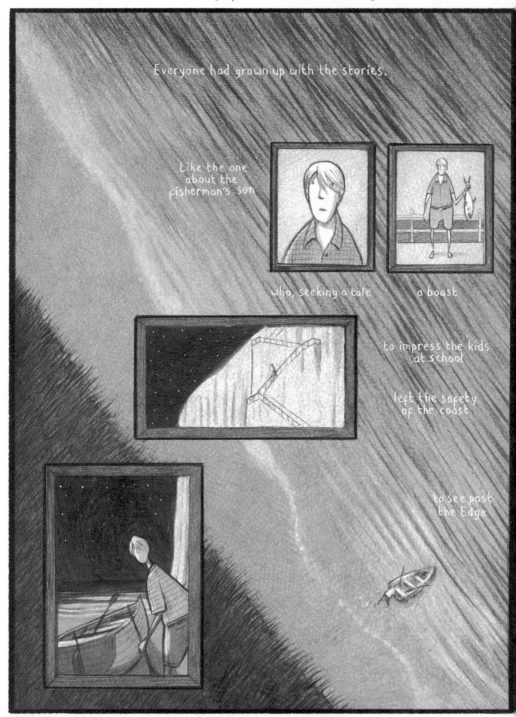

Everyone had grown up with the stories.

Like the one
about the
fisherman's son

who, seeking a tale

a boast

to impress the kids
at school

left the safety
of the coast

to see past
the Edge

They said
There

took his
tidiness
away.

Swallowed
his boundaries
whole.

Mixed his
right side

with his left side

his
insides

with his outsides

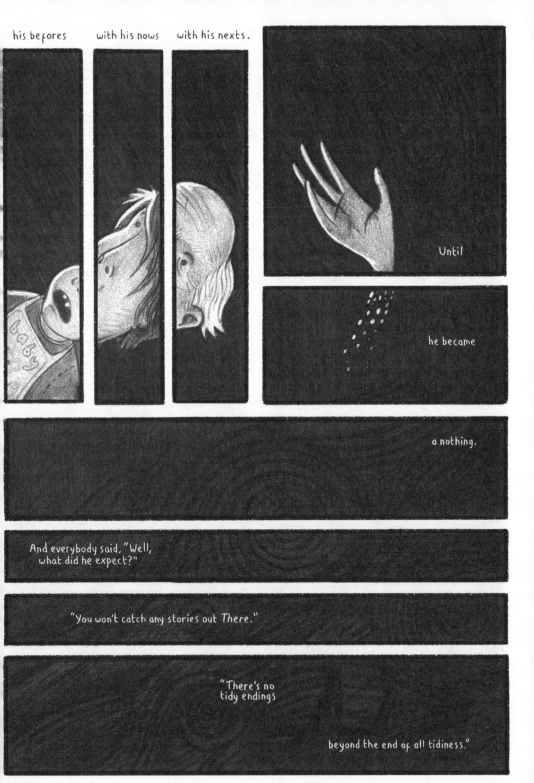

his befores   with his nows   with his nexts.

Until

he became

a nothing.

And everybody said, "Well, what did he expect?"

"You won't catch any stories out *There*."

"There's no tidy endings

beyond the end of all tidiness."

So you can see,
it was not strange for Dave

to ignore his sea view

and instead sketch every night
just the simple sight

of pedestrians,
post box

a neighbourhood cat or two...

It was, he felt
a way of keeping
a sense of order.

Of control.

Just his pencils,
his dinner,

and his drawings
of the street,

(and 'Eternal Flame' by The Bangles

on constant

constant

Eternal Flame
The Bangles

constant

REPEAT).

For after all, around Here,

ssssshh – ssssshh…

sssh – sssssh…

at the very edge of everything
at the very *end* of everything

everyone needs a trick.

A habit.

ssssh – ssssh… ssshh…

sssssssh – sssh… sssssh…

Something to block out the sound
that crashes all around

Something
predictable

and
familiar

to drown
all thoughts
of There.

Something, please God, to help ward off…

untidy dreams.

Mornings

were always a relief for Dave.

He *relished* the mornings.

and work was as far away from There

as it was possible to be.

Right in the very centre of Here.

	RECEIVED	SUBJEC
INBOX	Today 08:45	Today's Data
	Today 08:40	Today's Data
DRAFTS	Today 08:35	Today's Data
	Yesterday 17	Re: Today's Data

He liked the tidiness of numbers and charts

Please find attached the data
today's presentation.

Regards,
Ian Whithead - Data Analyst
Infosystems

A&C Industries Inc.
HERE-2067 (031-2996-28741

61321.dat

and the patterns of his day

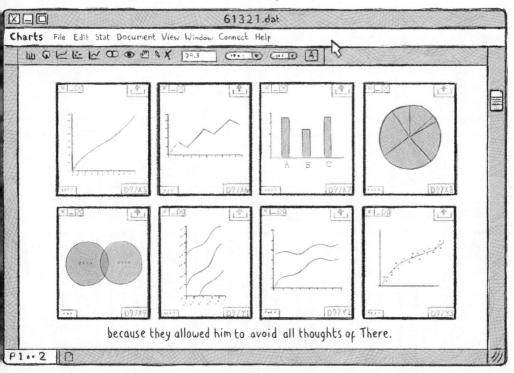

because they allowed him to avoid all thoughts of There.

(At least, for most of the time.)

It was only in the moments when he wasn't working that anxiety crept in.

Sometimes, for instance, Dave would wonder what it was his company actually *did*.

He'd wondered about this ever since he first started at A&C.

(Back in the pre-wig days)

Um...

What

What exactly does A&C industries... uh...

do?

Do?

Do?

Do?

Do?

Do?

Nobody really knew.

So Dave didn't ask again.

And every lunchtime, once he'd conveyed

all of the latest information

in his careful

brightly coloured

many-fonted presentation,

Dave was always left with a nagging question at the end:

And following this question, the familiar, disturbing suspicion

was fear.

Sometimes, Dave would sit in with his

  and he would listen to The Bangles

 and try to think

 of nothing.

But it didn't
always work.

For Dave, as for most people on Here,

there was never really any getting away from it.

The idea of There was always just

there.

Sitting, silently...

somewhere

through the invisible gaps

which connect

one moment

just to the left of vision.

Lacking form or precision.

Like...

...a weed.... that crawls up between the cracks...

to the next.

It was beneath the skin of things.

Behind the pattern of things.

It was under the streetlamp half-light

that the night-time brings.

It was
in the faraway song

that the
cold sea sings.

2.

THE HAIR

The hair

had always

always

always
been there.

It must have been the strangest, strongest hair in the world.

For whether it was shorn

plucked

snipped

ripped

or waxed,

within half an hour

it would always grow back.

Exactly the same as it was before.

In fact, the hair (as Dave had once said to Doctor Peterson)

had

He didn't notice it at first.

He didn't spot

CLICK CLICK

that the data which greeted him that day seemed unusually *random*.

The scatter charts in particular were more chaotic than normal.

A little too *scattered*.

For Dave, as ever

if the data was there,

that was all that mattered.

It was his boss who saw it first.

He'd come down with something

-fast-

as soon as he left Richmond's office.

gasp

It felt

not so much like sickness

as a kind of *dread*.

As if the chart he'd just seen had somehow

got inside his head.

As if something had escaped

from the depths of his dreams

to crawl up

into the day.

To bleed through the seams.

Dave, come on!

Outwardly, nothing seemed amiss.

Indeed, all witnesses concur that when Dave was finally coaxed from the booth,

At blimmin' last...

his face was perfectly

beautifully

girlishly smooth.

(Well, almost.)

And if what happened during Dave's presentation that afternoon

was the sort of thing

that *stories* are made of...

Hello Ladies,

gentle-men...

If it were possible

to connect

this to that

that to this.

and somehow show

a purpose,

or prove

some kind of pattern

BI-BIP

to the way things move...

But the problem is,

when something comes

from elsewhere

from a place beyond sense...

beyond tidiness...

beyond Here...

then, frankly...

...that's when
things get
messy.

there really is, in the end,

only one thing that can truthfully be said:

3.

THE BEARD

All night
long, Dave

and

and

Until, in the morning,

he finally gave up

CLICK

NEATNES

1. Failure to present to work in a state of perf
   in instant dismissal.

2. Failure of any employee to shave facial hair

TNESS DIRECTIVE

(It helped not to look back.)

He saw

what had been under his nose all along.

(Or, indeed, what hadn't.)

Perhaps the most disturbing

and remarkable story you've ever heard.

It is the story of a man whose face

has become, in just the past two days...

...a portal to *Hell*.

What

REC

REC

REC

REC

REC

Cut

What was that bit

Oh, nothing.

Hell. You said Hell.

That was just a bit of... colour. For the telly.

What?

You know. A bit of a story.

For the... research film.

Professor.

Would you mind telling me the story?

Perhaps before you tell the camera?

I want to know what's happening to me.

OK.

Do you have a pencil?

Soon enough Dave, who had for so long lived on the edge of things, became...

...the centre of attention.

Is that him?

Yeah

That's the bloke on the news

And as he tried to keep calm by sketching his view,

he found himself no longer drawing passers-by

but spectators instead.

The curious.

Oh my god...

Look at the size of that

The furious.

That's outrageous

Have a shave, man!

The watching.

And it would later be thought significant

that as the number of visitors grew

and grew,

nobody even thought of forming an orderly queue.

CLICK

UNBOLT

Dave tried to get rid of it for one last time

by feeding it

to the hungry brine.

ssssshh ʷʷʷʷʷʷʷʷ Isshhh...

It filled Dave's room.

It untidied his things.

And all he could do

was watch as it grew

And listen to it sing.

Is this burning...

... an eternal

ssssssh - sssssshh...

The **PARAMEDICS** were first.

Come on love

You'll be alright

Then

FIRE AND RESCUE

It's blunted the bloody bolt-cutters!

Then finally, the **POLICE**

Hold the kettle, chaps!

POLICE But it sought out the gaps. **POLICE**

and confounded them all.

The Here Mail

POLICE CAUGHT BY THE FUZZ

And even Dave – whose capacity for surprise was diminishing almost as fast as the beard was growing –

was amazed

by the speed with which the Army arrived on the scene

...with some sort of...

great big

tank-like

improvised machine...

BREAKING NEWS

He was also surprised

-DUGGA-DUGGA-DU

GA-DUGGA-DUGGA-DUGGA-   DUGGA-DUGGA-DUGGA-DUGGA-DUGG

A-DUGGA-DUGGA-*CLUNK*

by how quickly
it defeated them.

Its blackness seemed

to drown all thought.

People found themselves watching it for hours

as it curled into

and over

and around
itself.

It seemed to evade *definition* somehow,

for its top side
was its underside

its right side

was its
left side

and its inside
was its outside.

In fact, when people
looked at it closely,

they couldn't even
tell where it stopped.

Soon enough, observers reported strange psychological phenomena

such as
hypnosis

or a disconcerting feeling

of one's darkest,
most deeply buried
nightmares

migrating
to the surface

And strangest of all, a distinct sense

to the point where reality seemed to run...

They said:

It was
sort of like

trying to
read a story

but the pages
are all mixed up from
different books...

...so that it can't be read. Y'know?

and consuming trees

and attracting wildlife

...that the Government finally decided on more drastic action.

Three
months
later.

It had started out with 20.

By the end
of the week
it was 60.

In three months' time,
half the hairdressers of Here
had been conscripted.

The Government's
official line was thought up
by a hastily-appointed
consultant:

...the Beard Expert,
Professor Darren
Black

It's true, yes,
that it cannot
be physically
cut as such

But to be frank with
you Susan, it really is
simply a case of,
well...

If you can't
beat it,
style it!

But the results of the styling

were as much of a surprise to the hairdressers
as they were to everyone else.

People started asking them,

To which they could only reply,

to go *inland.*

And as all the people
of Here looked at
the Beard,

an uneasy
feeling of
recognition
formed.

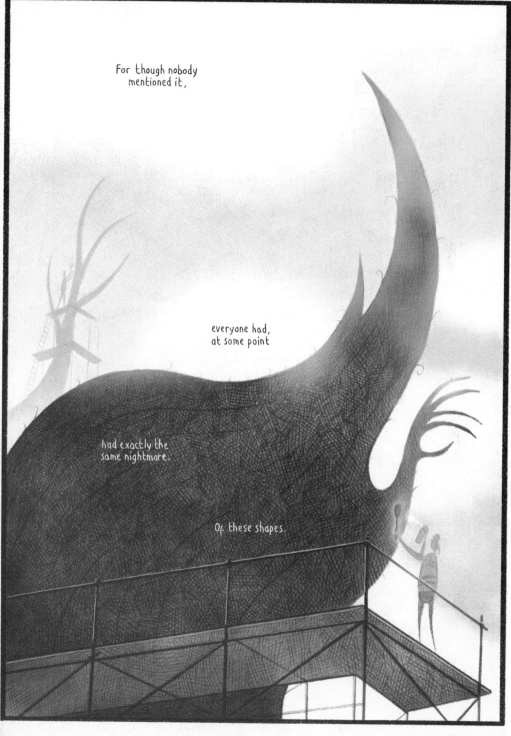

For though nobody
mentioned it,

everyone had,
at some point

had exactly the
same nightmare.

Of these shapes.

Of There.

All the while, at the bottom of the chaos

Dave just sat, with aching back

while drinking

a specially formulated,

supposedly beard-retarding,

NUTRITIONAL BREW

...and fielded
interview

after
interview

after
interview.

The Untidiness, as it later came to be known

first became apparent

in people's hairstyles.

For with all the *Hairdressers* now

CLOSED FOR BEARD DUTY

by government decree,

PUSH

everyone soon realised they would
have to cut their own hair –

SNIP
SNIP

There...

with differing results.

Consequently,
for the first time in his life

Dave found that
the people he drew outside his house

looked... not quite perfect.

And when there were no more
hairdressers to enlist,

the dog groomers were called in.

And when there were no more dog groomers,

the gardeners were summoned too.

Until, in the space of just four months

And ultimately,

what is the
act of *naming*,

but a special kind...

DO NOT CF

It had to end somewhere.

ROBIN
BASKINS bsc
Psychological
Services
Specialist in:
Nightmare removal
Teenager retraining
Braincycling
Interior Lifestyling
www.baskinspsy.here

NEWSPAPER OF THE YEAR

The Here Mail

P&insurance
est. 1879
Fire · Damage · Theft
Acts of Beard
Special Rate now available

Wednesday | All The Local News About The Things You Know | Today's weather: | 80p

SELF-GROOMING SPECIAL
Cut your own hair
Get this season's stubble
Untidy chic: how to do it right
only in today's **style**

PROPERTY
How can I Beard-proof my home?

WHY I'M ANGRY ABOUT ALL THIS
by Neil Putford
Here's voice of reason
bellows into the void

Government announces ambitious new Beard-management project

BALLOON PLAN FOR 'EVIL BEARD'

That's Not A Beard Idea: Project SkyHope will keep the beard hovering at a constant 300ft above ground level

by Stracie Gumton
Beard Correspondent

The Government has today announced a radical new plan to suspend the Giant Beard 300ft above West Here using a fleet of giant balloons.

The scheme, dubbed Project Sky-Hope, is intended to allay fears voiced by West Here residents that the Beard has become a permanent fixture in the region.

"It's merely a stopgap," said the popular psychologist and government Beard Advisor Professor Darren Black. "We hope to use a rotating fleet of 7-10 large balloons as a means of suspending the hair above housing stock and minimising scaffold footprint."

Reports of social disorder across Here have been attributed to the influence of the Beard, which campaigners believe is a mystical force of disruption from the Outer Realm.

The plan is predicted to be active for 6 weeks. "We anticipate that the Beard will begin to slow and eventually contract within that period, and until that happens we simply aim to suspend its mass above the rooftops, so as to minimise ground damage."

But the plan has already met criticism from the growing anti-Beard campaign, who are calling for the permanent removal of the Beard and its human originator.

Neil Putford of The Here Mail described the Beard as "a threat to all our lives and families, and perhaps even life as we know it".

A recent spate of untidiness has

"It is madness to keep it here," said Marco Grossman of North Here. "The longer it stays, the greater the infection of disorder and chaos throughout our society. If we do not see it go now, we will be witnessing the end of civilisation as we know it."

The conscription-led Hairdresser Shortage is believed to be at the root of the current disorder, though protestors claim that the phenomenon is more than a social trend brought about by circumstance.

"It is an invisible virus," said Penelope Winters, administrator of Mums Against Messiness (MAM). "You can't feel it, you can't see it, but it will infect you unless you kill the root cause."

Continued on Page 3

It was, of course, the Government's idea.

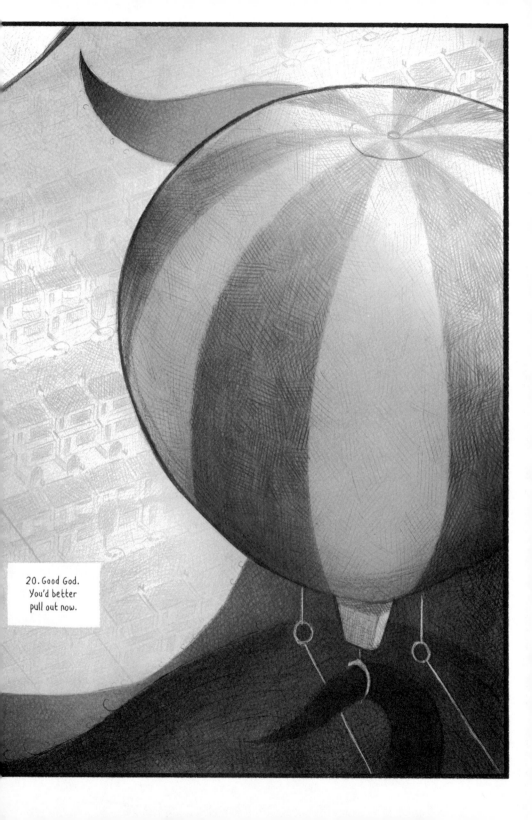

20. Good God.
You'd better
pull out now.

that there was

never any intention

n for anything other

than an indefinite process

s of low atmosphere Beard Suspension.

And all witnesses concur
that as the Beard began to lift

and the tethers began to

and

Dave looked

and he just took a last look
at his street

...do you feel my hear

and he said something so weird.

He said:

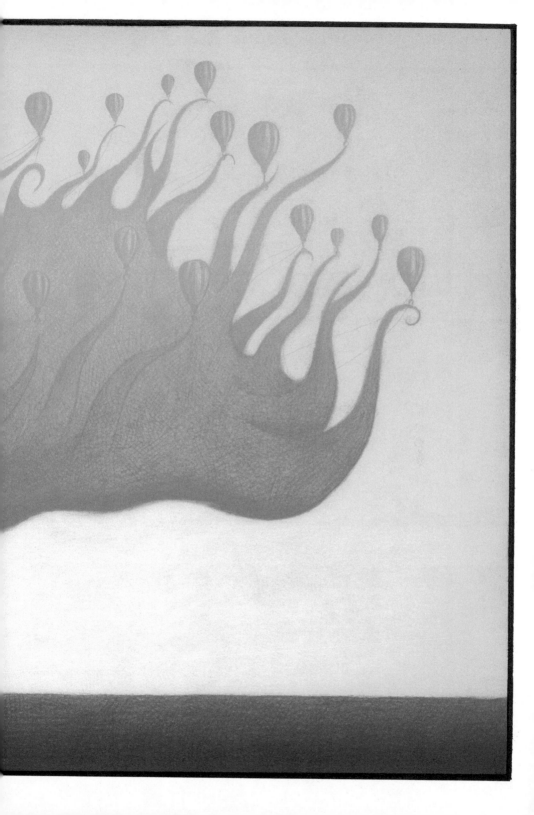

It wasn't pretty, that was true.

But it looked like an ending.

And as Dave sailed away

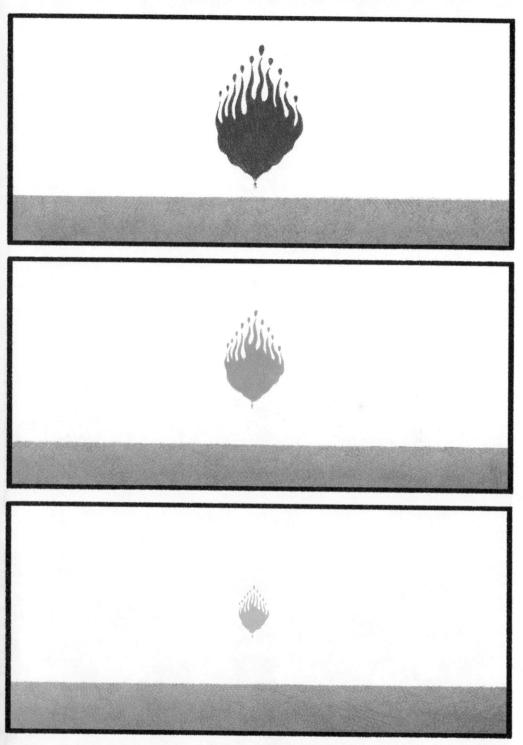

everyone knew:

The Beard Event
was over.

4.

THERE

#1 HEREWIDE BESTSELLER

The
THERE EQUATION

How a Little Bit of Chaos
Can Make Everything Much Tidier

by
Professor Darren Black
author of ETERNAL FLAME

"A fascinating book which basically
explains everything" – HERE MAIL

reads:

The changes were small at first.

For some, it began with a new self-administered hairstyle...

...which just kind of grew on them.

For others, it was a slightly less tidy 'look'...

...that just kind of stuck.

Pubescent sproutings
started growing

to become
movements

and clothing experiments

began to spawn unruly trends.

There was even a trickle of ex-beard spectators, who

having visited Dave's house
during the Event

found themselves
returning to the sea
for holidays

a little less afraid
than before.

The local architecture of the old Beard Zone also displayed changes,

where those who'd had
their houses destroyed by the Beard

found themselves

being
creative

with their insurance payouts.

And commuters who had once been forced

to try new routes to work

nowadays found themselves doing so

voluntarily.

It was the fear that people noticed most, though.

Or rather, its absence.

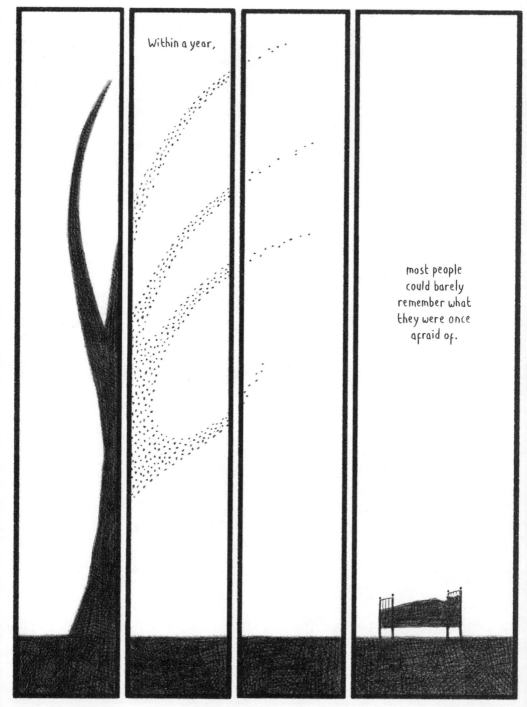

Within a year,

most people could barely remember what they were once afraid of.

And by the end of the decade,

it had almost become a lifestyle cliché

to, in the famous phrase of Professor Black,

Let a Bit of **There** Into Your Day!

"Yet another sort of... exercise video for the soul" TV Weekly

Professor arren Black

V TO BLU·RAY

Publicity max

And as the
years went by

with no further
Beard-like events,

what happened to Dave

The Eternal Flame Museum
Education Centre and Memorial Garden
to the Beard Event

Curator: Professor Darren Black

became *past.*

Nobody noticed

that this most extraordinary of happenings

had been absorbed

into the flow of life.

As familiar

as a well-known song.

A story

many times retold

Repackaged

and resold.

Reframed

Re-experienced

and ultimately reclaimed

by the inevitable growing-back

PLUCK

of the skin of things.

Today people no longer even see a scar.

But

Prof. Darren Black
Curator

finds
himself

more and more
aware

of There

KNOCK
KNOCK

Yes?

as the years fly past.

Some more on
the beach, Darren.

Very well,
Baz.

Let's go
fishing.

It will be written by the sea

ssssh...

>shake<

and by the skies

'Nuther one

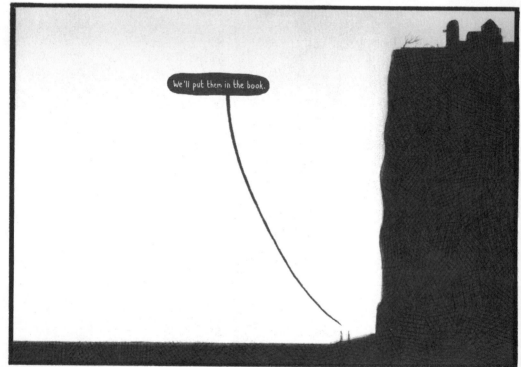

He hopes that one day

he might be able
to make some kind of sense

or sequence of
these images.

Maybe even a narrative.

A story from There.

So far, none is apparent.

1069B
W. Here   274B

1070B
W. Here   382D

1071B
East Here

1072B
N. Here   798C

1073B

Eat Here   497E

1074B

S. HERE   237B

1075B

W. HERE   274B

1076B

W. HERE   274B

1077B	
N. HERE	782Y

1078B	
South Here	958B

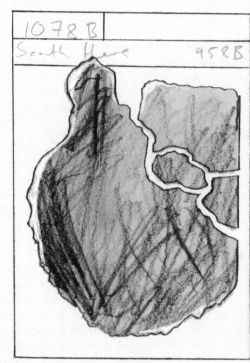

1079B	
W. HERE	682Y

1080B	
N. HERE	483E

1081B		1082B	
WEST HERE	432Y	E. HERE	241C

1083B		1084B	
EAST HERE	125E	N. HERE	429E

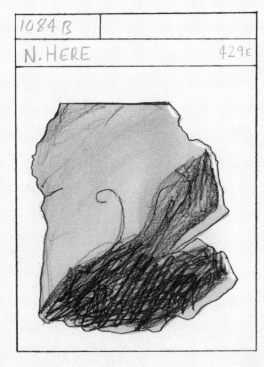

1085B	
W. Here	1934

1086B	
S. Here	128B

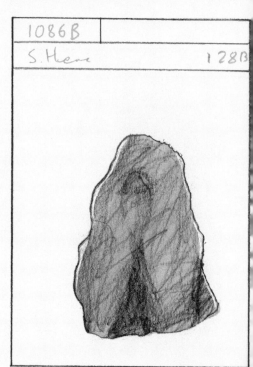

1087.B	
E. Here	149B

1088B	
E. Here	289B

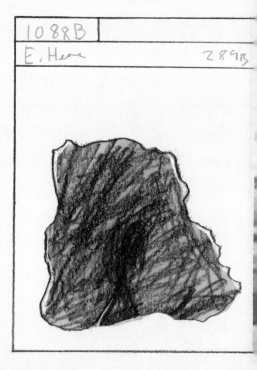

1089B		1090B	
S. Here	997B	S. Here	432B

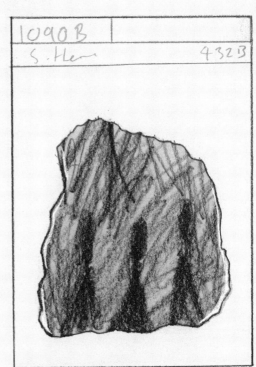

1091B		1092B	
West Here	459Y	W. Here	6794

1093B	
W. Here	273Y

1094B	
W. Here	193Y

1095B	
E. Here	655Y

1096B	
North Here	556B

1097 B		1098 B	
E. Here	249B	N. Here	658B

1099 B		1100 B	
South Here	199B	E Here	348B

Thank You

Alex Bowler and all at Jonathan Cape for
Beard-trimming and encouragement

Sam Copeland at RCW

My parents Margaret and Geoff Collins
for pretty much everything

Tony Illingworth and Maureen Rodger
for being inspirational teachers

Peter Brown, who commissioned my first cartoons
and encouraged me to keep at it

Tom Humberstone for showing me
what comics can do

Roger and Barbara Clarke
for letting me take over their office

And my wife Hannah - without
whose ideas, inspiration, editing,
support and endurance
this book would not exist.

STEPHEN COLLINS was born in 1980 and grew up in south London.
He began cartooning in 2003 and has since won several awards, including
the Jonathan Cape/Observer Graphic Short Story Prize and the inaugural
9th Art Award. His work has appeared in many publications worldwide,
including *Wired*, *GQ*, and the BBC, and he contributes regular comics to
The Guardian and *Prospect* magazine. He lives near Hertford with his
wife, his son, and a well-charged beard trimmer.

www.colillo.com

stephen-collins.tumblr.com

THE GIGANTIC BEARD THAT WAS EVIL. Copyright © 2013 by Stephen Collins. All rights reserved. Printed in the United States of America. For information, address Picador, 175 Fifth Avenue, New York, N.Y. 10010.

"Eternal Flame" words and music by Susanna Hoffs, Tom Kelly, and Billy Steinberg. Copyright © 1988 Bangophile Music. Universal Music Publishing Limited. All Rights Reserved. International Copyright Secured. Used by permission of Music Sales Limited.

www.picadorusa.com
www.twitter.com/picadorusa • www.facebook.com/picadorusa
picadorbookroom.tumblr.com

Picador® is a U.S. registered trademark and is used by St. Martin's Press under license from Pan Books Limited.

For book club information, please visit www.facebook.com/picadorbookclub or e-mail marketing@picadorusa.com.

The Library of Congress Cataloging-in-Publication Data is available upon request.

ISBN 978-1-250-05039-7 (paper over board)
ISBN 978-1-250-05040-3 (e-book)

Picador books may be purchased for educational, business, or promotional use. For information on bulk purchases, please contact Macmillan Corporate and Premium Sales Department at 1-800-221-7945, extension 5442, or write specialmarkets@macmillan.com.

Originally published in Great Britain by Jonathan Cape, an imprint of Random House Group Ltd.

First U.S. Edition: October 2014

10 9 8 7 6 5